Wroxeter Rom...

Roger H White

Contents

Tour of Wroxeter

OVERVIEW OF THE ROMAN TOWN

Before the Romans came to Britain, the site of Wroxeter had already been settled and turned into farmland under the control of the local tribe, the Cornovii. Their main settlement appears to have been the hillfort on the Wrekin, the hill to the east that dominates Wroxeter. Wroxeter was protected to the north and south by valleys of small streams and to the west by the river Severn, offering an attractive defensive location for a legionary fortress. The fortress also controlled a major ford across the river that allowed the Roman army to attack west and south, towards what is now Wales. The fortress was established as a base in the late 50s AD – first for the 14th Legion and then later for the 20th Legion. It was dismantled in the late 80s AD and the site was then handed back to the tribal authorities. We know from a wooden tablet found at Vindolanda near Hadrian's Wall that the Roman name for the fortress was 'Viriconium' and the town had the same name, with the addition of the tribal name, 'Cornoviorum' – 'Viriconium of the Cornovii'. By the fourth century it is possible that the name had changed to 'Uriconium', the name by which it is referred to in copies of late Roman documents that survived into the Middle Ages.

Above: Aerial view of the excavated remains of the Roman town, looking west. The baths are in the foreground and the recreated Roman town house (see page 18) is on the site of the forum. Beyond, the river Severn is in flood, demonstrating clearly why Wroxeter is on the higher, east bank of the river

Facing page: The Old Work, seen through the portico of the recreated town house

Today only the remains of the town's public baths can be seen, although from this central site, elements of the wider town and its setting can be appreciated. The remains consist of a fragment of wall, known as the 'Old Work', standing 7m in height, and the lower ruined walls of the baths and market hall. Where lost, walls have been replaced by pink concrete. The rooms themselves are marked out in different coloured gravels: coarse gravel for a road; red for a roofed but open walkway; and beige for inside a building. Areas that were once open are now grassed. A small museum contains an exhibition on the history of the site and displays some of the artefacts found here.

From the museum veranda, the line of the Roman street (the *decumanus*) can be seen in the foreground with the red gravelled covered walkway of the baths basilica beyond, and then the actual baths basilica building. The Old Work is a fragment of the south wall of this basilica. The modern road running past the museum lies above the town's main thoroughfare, Watling Street (the *cardo*), which was once three times the width it is now. This area was the centre of the Roman town. In the Roman period this setting was dominated by the major public buildings of the town, erected in the

Aerial view of the baths

1 Red gravel marks an open walkway round the baths basilica

2 Beige gravel indicates the inside of a building, in this case the baths basilica

3 Coarse gravel marks the line of the Roman street

4 The grassed areas, such as this space round the plunge pool, were once open

5 The Old Work

6 The main bath suite

7 Shops

8 Market hall

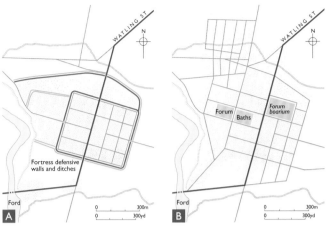

mid second century AD. In front of the museum veranda was the baths; on the other side of the road, where the recreated house and the Victorian labourer's cottage stand, was the forum. Behind and to the right, beneath the Victorian model farm, was probably the town's major civic temple (a colonnade was found here when the farm was built and geophysical survey has confirmed the presence of this feature on at least three sides). The modern crossroads adjacent to this farmyard was close to the central point of the town, one block north of where the *cardo*, the road running from north to south, crossed the *decumanus*, which ran from east to west. Surrounding these large and impressive civic buildings were town houses. We know from aerial photographs and geophysical survey, as well as from excavation, that there were large houses in this central area that looked similar to the recreated house. Beyond these areas, and especially to the north, over the crossroads, were the more industrial quarters alongside the houses of the less wealthy citizens. The view of these areas is obscured by the rising ground.

Other than the ruins at the centre of the town, there is very little visible of the large Roman town today. The main legacy is the roads, many of which follow the line of the streets of the Roman town. They include a green lane that once led out of the east gate of the town, taking traffic towards the Wrekin. This was used as a farm track until the 1970s. Recently, a 70-metre-long stone wall was identified on the ground here that might represent a fragment of a large walled compound, perhaps best interpreted as the town's livestock market – the *forum boarium*. At the edge of the town a modern fence line outlines the perimeter of the town's defences – a circuit of about three miles. At the moment much of the town is not accessible to the public, even though the land is owned or administered by English Heritage, since traffic makes it unsafe to walk along the roads within the walls to any great extent. It is hoped that in the future it will be possible to open up the site a great deal more to make these features more accessible.

The Development of Wroxeter Roman City

A *Wroxeter fortress (in red) between about AD 57 and AD 85. A bank and ditch north of the fortress shelters the settlement here and a construction compound lies between the fortress and the river. Civilians settled away from the fortress by the ford*

B *Wroxeter Roman City between about AD 85 and AD 180. At first the town had no defences and reused the fortress street grid*

C *Wroxeter Roman City between about AD 180 and AD 480. The mature town enclosed within its defences occupied an area of 78ha*

An aerial view of Wroxeter and
surrounding landscape, looking west

1 *Baths, town house and museum*
2 *River Severn*
3 *Line of the defences*
4 *Bell Brook*
5 *Watling Street and the site of*
  the cemetery
6 *St Andrew's Church*

THE EXTENT OF THE CITY

It is difficult to appreciate the full extent of the town from a single location as it is so large, but the viewing platform above the baths offers an excellent starting point. The ruins of the baths stand in a modern enclosure marked by a concrete post and chain-link fence. Beyond this is a large triangular field with the baths at the apex of the triangle. The broad base of the triangle, at the far side of the field, is the full length of the short side of Wroxeter's fortress. The modern road, with the baths on one side and the recreated town house on the other, marks the longer side of the fortress. This west side extends from the corner of this field, past the baths, the museum and its car park and ends just beyond the isolated house at the crossroads. Thus

this field and the ruins of the baths mark out the site of half of the former fortress. It is one of the few places in Britain where it is possible to appreciate in a single uninterrupted view the size of a Roman fortress. Yet the area of the town was once 78ha – four times that of the fortress. This one field represents one-eighth of the whole of the town's area. It is not possible to see the full extent of the town from the viewing platform; only about half of the town can be seen from here. Beyond the hedge line marking the short side of the fortress are the village of Wroxeter and its church, lying just inside the southern defences of the city; the church tower may be visible in the trees. The hedge behind the recreated town house stands on the river cliff that marks the western edge of the town.

Right: A full-size representation of the Roman baths at Xanten, Germany, in modern materials. The variety of roof heights and overall size gives a good impression of what Wroxeter's baths would have looked like

Below: Hot air circulated up the walls in the heated rooms, behind the plaster, through hollow box-flue tiles similar to this one

Bottom: View across the baths suite. The remains of the hypocaust, or underfloor heating system, is in the left foreground

▮ THE BATHS BASILICA

Wroxeter's bathhouse is a large and impressive example of a design that could be found in other towns across the north-western provinces of the Roman Empire. Because of the cooler climate here, the usual open-air exercise yard, found in Mediterranean countries, was not appropriate. Instead, a large open hall – the baths basilica – was provided. This was an impressive space, designed to awe the visitor; its appearance can easily be reconstructed at Wroxeter because of the survival of the Old Work. This wall, standing 7m high, was the south wall of the basilica. In front of it, in the yellow gravelled area, are round pink discs that mark where the columns of the basilica stood. These were as high as the Old Work and timber beams ran from them to the Old Work wall, supporting a sloping roof above. Above the columns stood another wall, the height and thickness of the Old Work but pierced at the upper level by large, round-headed windows. These shed light into the interior of the basilica, just as they do in a cathedral of similar design. Above this was the pitched roof of the basilica, its apex two and a half times the height of the Old Work, or about 18m.

Baths and Bathing in the Roman World

Almost every town in the Roman Empire had a public bathhouse. The baths seem to have been open to all – slave or free – although access was controlled by set hours. The poor bathed earliest, then women and then men, when the baths reached their best heat in the afternoon.

Going to the baths was not just about sanitation; it was about seeing and being seen. It was a place to relax and enjoy the company of friends but it was also where bathers could be shaved or have their hair cut in the latest Roman fashion. It was also an activity that took time: bathers had to exercise first to build up a sweat and then progress at their own pace through the unheated, warm and hot rooms, which could either be steamy or dry and hot. Here bathers could pay for a massage, play board games or chat to friends or clients and plan an evening meal, for which they would buy the ingredients in a neighbouring market, such as the one attached to the baths at Wroxeter.

Doctors often plied their trade at bathhouses because of the link established by

philosophers in this period between bathing and health. Manicure sets, stamps for eye salves and doctors' instruments have all been found at Wroxeter. Equally, religion played a part in Roman bathing, not least because people felt vulnerable while in the baths. This is why spa towns such as Bath were so important, as the hot springs there were seen as having a direct connection to the sacred world. Bathers would make offerings at the springs, including curses to ask the gods to punish those who had stolen goods from them, or votive eyes in metal or plaster, which could be offered in the hope of cures for ailments.

Above: A 19th-century watercolour of the Roman circular bath at Bath, by Sir Edward John Poynter. The hot springs at Bath were believed to have a direct connection to the underworld

Below: Strigils were used in Roman baths to scrape oil from the skin. This one was found at Wroxeter

Bottom left: Gold votive eyes, such as these found at Wroxeter, were offered to the gods as a cure for conjunctivitis – a result of poor bathing hygiene

Right: The Old Work today, seen from across the heated rooms

Below: Remains of Uriconium near Wroxeter, 1788, by the Revd Williams

▨ THE OLD WORK

The Old Work is an impressive survival in itself and it is easy to interpret how it was built and functioned. It is not clear why it survived but there is evidence that the rectangular room on its south side initially survived as a chapel and was then reused as a granary. The evidence for this comes from a number of burials found in the surrounding hypocaust system and from

Above: Holes in the Old Work, where wooden poles were inserted as it was being built. The wall was built up in horizontal courses; the bands of orange-red tiles helped strengthen the wall while the mortar set

Below: Diagram showing how the wall was built. Wooden poles were laid through the wall and used as scaffolding platforms

burnt grain found on the floor when it was first excavated. Such reuses of bath buildings are seen elsewhere in Britain and the Roman Empire (at the Jewry Wall in Leicester, for example, and in the Cluny baths in Paris).

The most prominent features of the Old Work are the double bands of orange-red tiles separated by neatly laid bands of stonework. On the north side, the face is plain, other than these alternating metre-high bands of stone and tiles. On the south side, the upper part of the wall has the scar of three equal-sized arches and projecting piers, indicating the shape of the lost roof of the room, a fragment of which lies next to the Old Work on the dark blue gravel (representing a cold-water pool). Also visible are regular rows of holes, often lying on the top layer of tiles. These were scaffold (putlog) holes and demonstrate how the wall was built. After the foundations were laid, the masons built the outer skins of the wall in stone, leaving a gap between, which was then filled with rubble and mortar. This was capped with a double layer of tiles which were long enough to go through the thickness of the wall and thus tied it together as the elements dried out. Work could then progress onto the next 'lift' of the wall. As the wall rose,

scaffold timbers were passed through the putlog holes so that masons could work on both sides at the same time. When the wall was finished, the timbers were pulled out and the holes were sealed with pink mortar. An example of this survives on the south side of the wall, above and to the left of the doorway. When the wall needed maintenance, the putlog holes could be reused. The wall was then mortared and plastered over and finished with a fresco scheme, so none of the banding was visible. Some of the mortar covering survives on the south side of the wall: just to the left of the doorway some of the original mosaic floor can be seen, preserved under this layer. The very wide opening, which contained two pairs of doors separated by a pier, shows just how strong this method of construction was: the width is far too great for a simple lintel to support and the wall only survives here because the construction is so strong.

Above: The worn stone threshold leading into the heated suites

Below: Part of the plaster vault from the entrance to the hot room, which would once have been sumptuously decorated

THE MAIN BATH SUITE (see plan on inside back cover)
The wide doorway leads into a rectangular space, the unheated room (known as the *frigidarium* **3**). On the south wall opposite, which now stands to one metre, were four doorways: two central ones and one in each corner. The central doorways are marked out by their stone doorframes and worn thresholds. Bathers went in the left-hand one, where oil was applied to their bodies, and progressed into the warm room (*tepidarium* **4**) and then into the hot, steamy *caldarium* **5**. The furnace for the *caldarium* can be seen at the far end of the complex, by the grassy slope ahead. The floor of these rooms is lost and all that can be seen is the remains of the pillars of tiles that once supported it, but a photograph taken in 1859 (see page 14) shows the last remnant of this floor; further fragments were found in the 1960s. Bathers then retraced their steps and exited into a sluice room, through the right-hand doorway and back into the *frigidarium*. Bathers could take an alternative route by passing through the corner doorways. These took bathers into symmetrically arranged secondary bath suites comprising a small rectangular warm room

(*tepidarium* **6**) and then a hot dry room (*sudatorium* **7**). The furnaces of these hot rooms are clearly visible, especially that on the eastern side, where the arched opening of the furnace can be seen on the way to the viewing platform. The small room with the tiled floor is now the only visible Roman floor in the complex. The sunken room next to it has a door or window and steps, providing access for the people who stoked the fires. The last element of the original baths was an open-air pool (*natatio* **8**) for bathers to use as an outdoor plunge pool.

Above: A reconstruction of the interior of the baths basilica as first built. In the main hall, people exercise before going into the baths. In the aisles, hairdressers and eye doctors practise their trade while, at the end of the hall, a statue of Fortuna Balnearis protects the bathers. Men and women may well have bathed at the same time, although we cannot be certain of this

Left: The natatio, *an open-air plunge pool*

Above: The baths in 1859, when much of the standing remains of the hypocaust survived

Below: The baths today, taken from the same viewpoint as the photograph above. Nothing remains of the hypocaust visible in the Victorian photograph

THE STATE OF THE RUINS

The ruins of the baths have now been exposed for over 150 years and as a result they are poorly preserved. In places, the walls have had to be rebuilt from the ground up, as is shown by the modern tiles at ground level. The changes are best seen by comparing photographs taken in 1859, when the baths were first excavated, with the site today. While the walls were buried, the lime mortar holding them together washed away and was replaced by earth. When uncovered, the ruins simply fell apart. The tile stacks were also weak and did not survive the attentions of Victorian souvenir hunters for long.

Conservation work began in the 1950s, lasting for 20 years. The site was restored to look as it did when it was first uncovered. The rebuilding has made it difficult to distinguish the different phases of the baths but it is clear that the western baths suite was extended to fill the gap between the main suite and the latrine in the third or fourth century, at about the time when the *natatio* was filled in.

There is some evidence too that the main baths suite was abandoned and the building stone robbed out, perhaps as early as the fourth century. This may have been because it was too expensive to heat or repair and it proved more sensible to cannibalize the materials from these rooms to expand the smaller bath suites. The remains of the blocking of the doorways from the *frigidarium* into the main bath suite can still be seen in one doorway but are shown more clearly in a Victorian photograph. There were evidently problems with

heating the large rooms of the main suite, because a furnace was later added (below the modern viewing platform) which provided direct heat into the *tepidarium*. A thick sandstone wall was also built round the outside of the baths, which may have acted as insulation for the underfloor heating system, slowing heat loss from the rooms. Heating these rooms would have been a huge burden on the town's finances. The move to suites of smaller, more easily heated rooms would have provided a ready solution to the problem and may even have allowed men and women to bathe at the same time.

9 LATRINE

The three rooms between the baths and the modern street were designed at the same time as the baths, although they were separate from them. The largest was the latrine, identifiable by the long, deep drain running parallel to the red-gravelled portico, or covered walkway. A gap in the corner marks the doorway. Another door in the south wall of the basilica allowed people to access the latrine from there. No internal fittings survive other than the drain. This would have run continually with water draining from the baths – the only visible part of the town's extensive water supply.

WATER SUPPLY

The water for the town was diverted from the Bell Brook stream. It flowed into a clay-lined channel cut into the ground that ran down the hillside at a gently sloping angle, delivering the water into a large cistern situated inside the defences at the highest point of the town, north of the ruins of the baths. From there the water was conducted by gravity in a buried channel – visible in aerial photographs – to the baths to fill the pools. To keep the water fresh – important in a heated bathhouse, where stagnant water would quickly grow poisonous algae – it was never turned off and so continually flushed the latrine drain, flowing then into the smaller latrine in the market hall and then running alongside the forum and finally emptying into the river.

Left: Aerial view of Wroxeter with the Wrekin beyond. The baths, town house and farm are visible at the bottom of the image. Prominent are Watling Street **1** *, the Bell Brook, source of the town's water supply* **2** *and the road heading from the baths towards the Wrekin* **3**

Below: A third-century depiction of a fruit and vegetable shop from Ostia, Italy. Wroxeter's market stalls might have been similar to this

A Market Stall

'Here, hunger is costly, and the *macellum* ruins us.'
(Martial, *Epigrams*, Book 10, 96.9)

🔟 SHOPS

The two square rooms with central piers faced out onto the wide portico and the street. There is no visible clue to their function but they clearly had wide openings that were probably closed with wooden shutters. The piers supported a vaulted roof and rooms above. These were probably bars or shops selling refreshments, where bathers could get a drink or a meal as part of their visit to the baths. It is possible that doctors saw patients above these shops. Travellers passing through the town or using the forum opposite would also have been grateful for somewhere to get refreshments.

1️⃣1️⃣ MARKET HALL AND FORUM

The *macellum* or market hall formed an important part of the baths complex. It provided somewhere for the bathers to get food for their evening meal, and the shop rents would have helped pay for the running of the baths. The main entrance to the market hall was from the portico facing onto the street, rather than from the baths. The regularly sized open-fronted shops, arranged around three sides, opened onto an internal courtyard. A narrower room on one side is the site of a staircase up to a first floor; the rooms on this floor, which may not have been open to the public, must have been accessed by a corridor. An L-shaped room in one corner of the building is a latrine. Finds of bone suggest that goods on sale in this market hall are likely to have been high-quality cuts of meat, shellfish, fish and game rather than trinkets or jewellery. It is likely that the prices in the market were quite high – certainly that is the complaint made about such markets elsewhere in the Empire, most notably by the Roman poet and satirist Martial.

Across the road was the forum, an important building, combining the functions of a market, town and county hall and magistrates' court. The imposing street façades were colonnaded, and this is the only element visible today. (Apparently deeply buried, this colonnade lies on second-century ground level, which shows how much soil has accumulated at Wroxeter over nearly two millennia.) The main side, facing onto Watling Street, had a prominent entrance that carried a fine inscription dedicating the building to the Emperor Hadrian and dating its completion to AD 129–30 (see page 32). A row of shops also faced onto the street on this side, taking advantage of passing trade. Beyond the doorway was a large courtyard, presumably full of stalls on market day. On the far side was a huge basilica, identical in size and design to the baths basilica. This was where business was conducted, including legal business; cases were heard by judges seated on a raised tribunal at one end of the hall. Beyond the main hall were the offices of those responsible for running the affairs of the town and the tribe. If Wroxeter followed the conventional Roman civic model, these rooms included the offices of the two

Left: The remains of the colonnade of
the forum
Above: Bone gaming counters found
at Wroxeter. Gambling was a popular
Roman pastime

Below: Samian ware vessels, mixing
bowls and whetstones found in the
gutter of the forum

elected magistrates, the record office, the treasury and the
shrine. It is likely that the town's main temple was located
elsewhere – probably beneath the Victorian farm buildings
opposite the museum.

Markets were generally held on a nine-day cycle, although
the exact arrangements are unknown. Goods of all kinds were
on sale, including items made in the town as well as those
brought in from elsewhere.

Fire in the Forum

In about AD 170 there was a
fire in the forum. A stall,
complete with goods, fell
into the gutter. When
archaeologists found it, they
discovered that it included a
consignment of unused glossy
red Samian ware vessels; a
batch of white mixing bowls
(*mortaria*), used in the
kitchen to grind foodstuffs;
and bundles of whetstones
for sharpening knife blades.
This one stall provided clear
evidence of a Roman trade
network, since the Samian
ware had been made in
central Gaul (in the
Puy-de-Dôme region). These
vessels had been transported
to London, where the
Kentish ragstone whetstones
were added to the load, and
then sent up Watling Street,
where the *mortaria* were
collected, at Mancetter in
modern Warwickshire.

THE RECREATED HOUSE

In 2010, a version of a Roman town house (a *villa urbana*) was built by six modern-day builders using only tools and materials known to the Romans, for the television programme 'Rome Wasn't Built in a Day'. The costs of construction were met by the production company, while English Heritage provided a suitable location and monitored the building work. The new house comprises a street frontage with its portico and a lock-up shop. Behind the façade are a row of rooms and a bathing suite at right angles forming a courtyard. The villa does not have any foundations, other than a raft of compacted rubble, so as not to damage the underlying archaeology, which remains undisturbed.

Design

The design of the Roman town house at Wroxeter is loosely based on a house (Wroxeter site VI) which was excavated by JP Bushe-Fox between 1913 and 1914. This house had a long and complex development. It was originally three separate buildings which fronted Wroxeter's main street. These were then combined to form an L-shaped building similar to the new town house, with rooms around a courtyard and a separate bath complex. The recreated town house, designed to resemble a third- or fourth-century house, includes elements of this plan; its design was developed by Professor Dai Morgan Evans from the University of Chester.

Interior

The recreated house has few exterior openings, as is common in Roman town houses. A single room opening onto the street

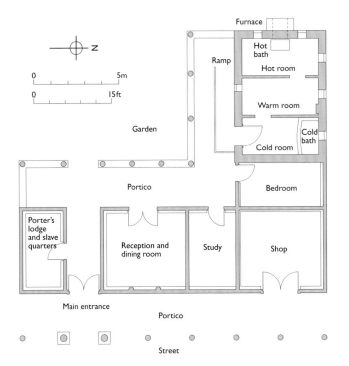

Furnace

Hot bath

Ramp

Hot room

Warm room

Garden

Cold bath

Cold room

Portico

Bedroom

Porter's lodge and slave quarters

Reception and dining room

Study

Shop

Main entrance

Portico

Street

N

0 ⊕ 5m
0 15ft

Left: Plan of the recreated town house
Below: Painted wall plaster from Verulamium – Roman St Albans. The wall-paintings in the recreated town house use the same bold colour scheme, but contain lively portraits of the modern-day builders, giving visitors a clue as to the origins of the house

portico operates as a lock-up shop in the north-east corner of the house and a wooden door, framed by hand-carved stone pillars, provides the principal entrance to the house from the street. Rooms are entered from the corridor around the courtyard and display a variety of finishes according to their status and use. Thus the first room is the doorkeeper's room, with its functional decoration, while the principal reception and dining room is the most lavishly decorated with a mosaic and frescoed walls. The neighbouring room has been left partly finished to demonstrate construction techniques. The bath suite is heated by a furnace on the west side of the building. From here hot air circulates under the raised floors of the hypocaust and up the walls of the warm and hot rooms through hollow box-flue tiles. The first room is unheated and contains a cold bath.

Above: The courtyard garden in the house of the Vettii, Pompeii. Roman houses often had courtyard gardens where flowers and herbs were grown

Garden

A Roman household would have used the courtyard for exercise and conversation. Flowers and culinary herbs may have been grown there. The surrounding portico provided shelter from the weather, both for the family and also for servants and slaves, who could have used it as a covered workspace.

Occupants

The owners of the excavated town house (site VI) seem to have accumulated their wealth gradually, since they invested it in making improvements to their house over an extended period. In the recreated house, income could have been generated by letting out the self-contained corner shop to a tenant, as was common. This tenant might be a former slave of the household, who had purchased his freedom. Tradesmen in Roman towns would have lived in smaller houses with narrow street frontages, which provided workshop and living space behind a shop. The recreated town house is more substantial and the owners of a property like this may well also have owned a villa and farmed land outside the town.

Methods

The site chosen for the experiment was above the forum of Roman Wroxeter. To protect the archaeology that still remains buried here, a one-metre high platform was laid down to act as a foundation for the new house. Where possible, the builders only worked with tools and technologies available to the Romans. Their guide was the ten-volume construction manual *De Architectura*, written by the Roman engineer Vitruvius some time after 26 BC. Modern legislation demanded some compromises, as did the small size of the team and a tight timetable and budget.

Materials

As in the Roman period, the materials used for the project were sourced locally, where possible. Sandstone was used for the fire-resistant bath suite, but the rest of the house was built on low stone walls that supported a timber frame – a technique widely used in Roman Wroxeter's buildings. A variety of materials was used to fill in the frame, including wattle and daub and mud bricks, which were faced in lime plaster to protect them from the weather. The portico facing the street includes two stone columns emphasizing the entrance, but the others are shaped and painted tree-trunks; both wooden and stone columns would have been used in the Roman buildings at Wroxeter. The roofs are made of tiles or wooden shingles and the floors are made of beaten earth (in one case mixed with ox blood). The builders manufactured their own box-flue tiles to line the hypocaust; other components had to be bought in because of a shortage of time.

Builders

In Roman times, labour was plentiful and cheap. This town house, however, was built by a core team of six modern builders with a range of skills, who were sometimes supplemented by local volunteers. Surveying was done using a *groma*, a simple instrument the Romans used to lay out straight lines and angles; timbers and stone were both shaped by hand; and human muscle-power took the place of cranes and wheelbarrows, as it would have done in Roman times. As well as avoiding modern power tools and technologies, the builders had to turn their hands to many different tasks, including the mosaic and wall-paintings, which in the Roman period would have been the work of highly skilled specialists.

The Finished House

The building offers important lessons about houses in Roman towns. The constraints of the project and its timetable, together with the limited labour force, emphasized the fact that plentiful, cheap labour would have been essential for work such as this. The project demonstrated too the amount of material needed for such a house, which would have been a considerable investment. Thirty-six tonnes of lime was used in this building and ten tonnes each of stone and timber. It is sobering to realize that more than 100 examples of this type of building are known in Wroxeter. Despite the difficulties, the resulting structure gives a good sense of what a comfortable town house on the edge of the Roman Empire might have been like. Even only partly furnished, Wroxeter's villa is a powerful evocation of what it was like to live in a Roman town house.

Above: The exterior of the recreated house. The portico includes two stone columns, emphasizing the entrance; the other columns are shaped and painted tree-trunks

Below: A replica of an altar to the Roman sun god Sol Invictus, built into the front wall of the house

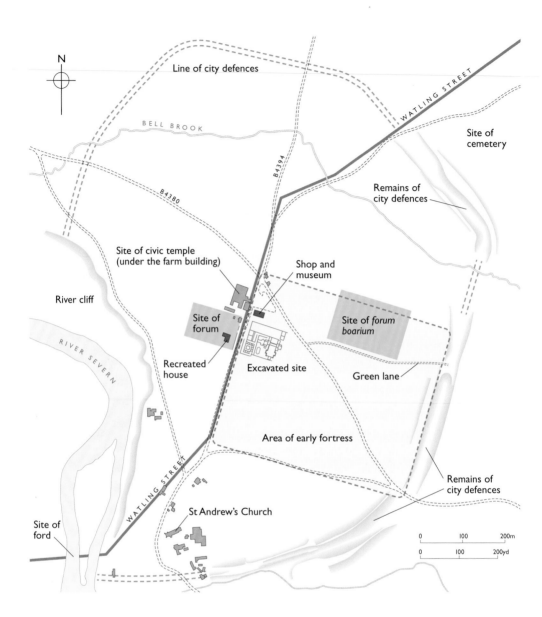

Above: Plan of Wroxeter Roman city, showing the line of the defences and the position of the fortress

THE OUTER DEFENCES

Unlike many Roman towns in Britain, Wroxeter never seems to have had impressive stone defences. Instead, the town seems to have been defined and defended by earth banks and ditches, much like an Iron Age hillfort. These were constructed at the end of the second century – a time when many towns in Roman Britain were building stone or earth defences. We know of no reason why towns felt that they had to have defences at this time, since Britain does not appear to have been threatened. Towns built defences for other reasons, however: town walls in the Roman period, as in the Middle Ages, were a status symbol as much as a practical means of defence. The walls also enabled those ruling the town to control access to the markets, and thus raise taxes on goods imported and sold there. Whatever the reason, the decision to build defences meant undertaking a large construction project, perhaps using labour recruited from the Cornovii tribe, whose capital Wroxeter was. The circuit is nearly three miles in total and at first comprised a bank with a clay and rubble core and a timber palisade on top. Two ditches were dug in front of the wall, with a gap left where the roads led into the town. The defences were renewed, perhaps in the fourth century, by digging a very large single ditch through the line of the two earlier, shallower ditches, and heightening the bank. The bank and the edge of the inner ditch were aligned so that they formed a single continuous slope, six or seven metres high. A well-preserved section of the defences can be seen from the car park of the Wroxeter Hotel in the village. There is some evidence that a slighter stone wall with a bank behind it was built on the river cliff, where a ditch was unnecessary.

Above: The font in St Andrew's Church is carved out of the base of a Roman column
Below: Roman columns from Wroxeter reused as gateposts at St Andrew's Church

ST ANDREW'S CHURCH

The modern village of Wroxeter lies mostly within the limits of the Roman town, the boundary being formed here by a small brook running down to the river Severn. The Church of St Andrew is situated just inside the defences, directly opposite the road leading from the ford across the river, now the private drive to Boathouse Cottage. Roman stone has been reused in the churchyard wall and two Roman columns with weathered capitals support the cast-iron gate, erected in the 1860s. St Andrew's, which is in the care of the Churches Conservation Trust, is a notable example of a church displaying work from many different historical periods. Highlights include a Saxon north wall, built with large Roman stone blocks; a Norman chancel with a blocked priest's door; and the fragments of a ninth-century Anglo-Saxon cross built into the south wall when it was realigned in the mid 18th century. The field across the road from the church has produced evidence for early Roman settlement, perhaps focused on the ford, while a neighbouring field contains the prominent earthworks of a medieval manor house and its fishponds.

History of Wroxeter

INTRODUCTION

For much of its history, Wroxeter has been farmland, but during the Roman period it became the fourth largest town in Britannia after initially being a fortress. It acted as the tribal capital of the Cornovii, who controlled much of what is now Shropshire and Cheshire. Unusually, there is evidence that the city survived into the sixth or seventh century but then rapidly dwindled to become a typical English village with a church, manor house and farms. In the Victorian period, the Roman remains began to be excavated at about the same time that a model farm was established.

THE ARRIVAL OF THE ROMAN ARMY

When the Roman army moved into the Wroxeter area in the mid 40s AD, shortly after the invasion under the Emperor Claudius, they found a landscape that was already extensively farmed and settled. The land had been cleared for agriculture in the mid Bronze Age (perhaps about 1500 BC) as is shown by the discovery of Bronze Age pottery and burial mounds beneath the town. In the Iron Age, from about 800 BC to the Roman conquest, the land was occupied by small farmsteads enclosed by simple ditches. It is possible that the owner of one of these farms – Viricio – gave his name to the new town. Alternatively the name Viriconium could have come from the ancient name for the Wrekin – the hill which overlooks the site.

The Roman army came to Wroxeter from two directions: on one side, they followed the course of the river Severn, as marked by temporary fortresses at Leighton and Cound on either side of the river; and on the other side – the main attack route – they came from the north of the Wrekin, along what

Above: Late Iron Age pot found at Wroxeter, dating from the time of the early fortress
Below: Roman soldiers building a fort, as depicted on Trajan's Column in Rome in the second century AD. The Roman army moved into the Wroxeter area soon after the invasion of Britain in the mid 40s AD

Facing page: Detail from The Fall of Uriconium *by Thomas Prytherch, a Victorian local artist – a dramatic depiction of the end of Roman rule at Wroxeter*

Right: Reconstruction drawing of Agricola, governor of Britain from AD 77 to AD 85, leaving Wroxeter with his troops to campaign in northern Britain in AD 79

Below: Tombstone of Tiberius Claudius Tirintius, a cavalryman in a Thracian cohort, who may have been a member of the garrison at Wroxeter

became in the 19th century Thomas Telford's London to Holyhead road. The army apparently conquered the tribe easily, although there must have been some resistance as the Wrekin hillfort was attacked and burnt. The ferocity of this attack may have been enough to compel the tribe to surrender.

The Romans initially built a small fort in the late 40s AD for a cavalry unit of 500 men south of the present village; a tombstone was found there of Tiberius Claudius Tirintius of a Thracian cohort, who may have been a member of the garrison. About a decade later a more commanding site nearby was found for the fortress. This site was protected by the river Severn and offered uninterrupted views of the landscape with its surrounding hills, the location of the former tribal hillforts.

WROXETER AS A ROMAN FORTRESS

Roman fortresses followed very similar plans wherever they were built. This was so that any soldier serving in the legions would know where particular buildings were located, even if he had never been to that fortress before. The Roman army relied largely on foot soldiers. A legionary fortress would contain a legion of about 5,000 foot soldiers, who were all Roman citizens, and only 500 or so cavalrymen, who were usually recruited from other tribes. Soldiers could march 20 miles a day when on campaign and were professional soldiers. In return for

signing up for 25 years' service, soldiers were paid and were given good regular meals, excellent medical services (for the time) and career prospects. It is little wonder that service in the legions was sought after.

Barracks

Both auxiliary forts, holding 500 or 1,000 men, and legionary fortresses, holding 5,500 men, followed the same playing-card shape: rectangular with rounded corners. The defences of earth and timber had a ditch in front for protection and drainage; the army surveyors were careful to choose healthy sites to locate their fortresses. Latrines and cooking areas were located on the back of the ramparts to minimize health risks.

The barrack blocks occupied much of the interior space. Each barrack could accommodate 80 men and their officers. The men were housed in ten rooms – each room, known as a *contubernium*, held eight men. Letters found at Vindolanda Fort, near Hadrian's Wall, demonstrate that the men in these units were clearly very close to one another, referring to each other as 'brother'. On campaign the same group would share a tent. Non-commissioned officers, the centurion and *optio* had more roomy quarters at the end of the barrack block. None of the men was allowed to have his wife and children with him but families were permitted to live outside the fortress in a village,

Below: The remains of the granary at Housesteads Fort on Hadrian's Wall. The fort at Wroxeter would also have had a granary to supply the troops

known as the *vicus*. Marriage to a Roman soldier was attractive,
as a soldier's wife and children would then become Roman
citizens. We know of three Roman soldiers from Wroxeter's
garrison whose tombstones are in Shrewsbury. Titus Flaminius
of the 14th Legion was an eagle-bearer (*aquilifer*) with 22 years'
service; Marcus Petronius was a soldier also of the 14th Legion;
and Caius Mannius Secundus was a clerk (*beneficiarius*) to the
commander of the 20th Legion, with 31 years' service. All came
from northern Italy.

Officers' Houses

Officers (*tribunes*) lived in Roman-style houses on the main
street of the fortress, the *via praetoria*, while the commander
(*legatus*) had a grand house (the *praetorium*), in the centre of
the fortress, next to the headquarters building (the *principia*).
These men were drawn from the Roman aristocracy and were
expected to serve only for a few years in the legions before
taking on political, judicial and administrative roles in the
Empire. They were allowed to have their families and slaves
with them. The most famous legate known to have served at
Wroxeter was Gnaeus Julius Agricola, father-in-law of the
Roman historian Tacitus, who wrote his biography, *Agricola*.
Tacitus tells us that Agricola began his campaign of conquest
with an attack first on north Wales and then northern Britain. It
is likely that he launched his attack from Wroxeter, since this
was the base of the 20th Legion, with whom he had once
served. Within six years, he had extended Roman territory into
the Scottish lowlands and up the east coast as far as Inverness.

Governor of Britain
'Agricola became great
and famous as one who,
when entering on his
province, a time which
others spend in vain
display and a round of
ceremonies, chose rather
toil and danger.'
(Tacitus, *Agricola*, 18)

Communal Buildings

The *principia* was the administrative, financial and religious
centre of the fortress and was the first building laid out when
the fortress was planned. It was always an impressive building

and would have been clearly visible to anyone standing on the surrounding hills. Nearby would have been a hospital (*valetudinarium*), storehouses and granaries (*horrea*). Workshops (*fabricae*) were also essential, allowing the soldiers to make and repair armour and weapons and shoe the horses used by the cavalrymen. An annexe containing kilns and areas for livestock was located between the river and the west wall of the fortress. A bathhouse was under construction here when the army left the site in the late 80s AD.

We know of two garrisons using Wroxeter fortress: the 14th and 20th Legions. At first the fortress would have been a fully functional fighting base – the headquarters of the legion while it rested between campaigns in Wales. As the Roman army's attacks moved further north, however, Wroxeter's relevance declined and eventually it was no more than a fortified store depot.

The Cornovii

In common with other Iron Age tribes, the Cornovii lived both in hillforts and in lowland farmsteads. The extent of the tribe's lands is unknown but apparently included much of Shropshire and Cheshire. Finds from these sites are scarce but include prestigious items such as swords, brooches and horse equipment. They did not, however, use coins, unlike some of the Iron Age tribes of southern Britain. Surprisingly pottery was rarely used other than as containers for transporting salt, a vital commodity for the tribe, which seems to have been heavily reliant on livestock, and especially cattle, as its main resource. Salt was used to preserve meat, make cheese, and tan leather.

The discovery of a well-constructed Iron Age road west of Wroxeter implies a wider road and trade network, hinting at the relative

sophistication of the tribe, despite the lack of artefacts.

The Roman arrival in Cornovian territory must have been shocking but the tribe would not have suffered too greatly as the Cornovii quickly surrendered. They would have had to learn how to use money and get used to the concept of buying things rather than trading

Below: Tombstone of a Cornovian woman who married a Roman soldier, from Ilkley Roman Fort

them. Archaeologists have found coins and pottery belonging to the native tribe to the south, the Dobunni, suggesting that they brought their own coins with them to trade with the Romans. Pottery and many other goods were made by the army, or imported, and the Cornovii would have used these too.

Communication was perhaps less of an issue: both natives and Romans are likely to have spoken or understood the native language, a predecessor of Welsh and related to ancient European Celtic languages, but the natives would have had to learn Latin if they wanted to progress in society. Over time, people got used to the Roman army. We know of at least one Cornovian woman who married a soldier and was buried at a fort in Ilkley, Yorkshire.

Right: A street in the ancient Roman town of Herculaneum, lined with the remains of shops and houses
Below: An inscribed bronze tablet, found in the forum basilica at Wroxeter, issued on 14 April AD 135, during the reign of the Emperor Hadrian. It records the award of citizenship to Mansuetus, a cavalryman who served in the second cohort of the Dalmatians

Facing page: View through the Old Work, looking south-west

DEVELOPMENT OF THE TOWN

When the Roman army abandoned Wroxeter's fortress to relocate to Chester, they levelled the defences but left some of the buildings intact along with the street grid. These formed the nucleus of the new town. The population would have been drawn from local people – traders who had moved to the area from the territory to the south and some veteran soldiers who chose to settle in the area. One such veteran appears to have owned a farm at Duncote, a mile north of Wroxeter, because there was a small farmstead here with fields, each of which was one Roman acre in size – ideal for growing cash-crops to sell in Wroxeter's market.

We have no record of the town's administration but it probably followed the normal pattern of a council (*ordo*) elected by landowning men of the town and tribe, with two annual magistrates chosen from among this group. These men were responsible for tax gathering on behalf of the state, local justice and administration and the observance of official religious cults. The provincial governor would have visited the town on an occasional basis to dispense justice in more serious cases. To serve on the *ordo* you had to be a local landowner, which meant that most of its members came from the local tribal aristocracy, but there would also have been a small number of army veterans who lived in the town and they too would have been eligible, as they were Roman citizens. An inscribed bronze tablet recording the discharge of some Roman cavalrymen was found in a room in the forum basilica when it was excavated in the 1920s.

One of the first decisions of the *ordo* would have been to determine the boundary of the town (its *pomerium*). This was important as it also established where it was possible to bury the dead, as burial within the sacred town boundary was not permitted in Roman law. The council ambitiously chose to establish a town of 48 blocks covering four times the area of

Above: This inscription was once over the entrance to the forum. It dedicates the building to the Emperor Hadrian (r.117–138). It was only uncovered in the 1920s and the town's name was finally confirmed

Below: Aerial view of Wroxeter. The Roman city once extended out into the countryside

the fortress (approximately 78ha or 180 acres), slightly larger than the town of Pompeii in Italy. The costs for constructing the town and its civic buildings fell on the tribe. Taxes were raised locally by the town council, so the size of the town tells us something of the wealth of the tribe as they perceived it.

Where possible the new street grid was an extension of the fortress but in places the lie of the land made this impossible (see plans on page 5). For instance, the new town included the valley of the Bell Brook, the source of its water. In parts this valley has steep sides and it would have been impossible to build on these. Lower down the valley, it opens out so that it was possible to lay out streets across the Bell Brook, aligned on the brook itself and at an angle to the rest of the grid. As a result, the centre of the new town shifted: it now lay on a street running north–south through the centre, overlying the former western defences of the fortress. The baths and forum were established on either side of this street, with the town's temple perhaps on an adjacent grid. The main east–west street ended at a very large town house on the river cliff, perhaps home to the tribe's most important family.

The streets extended out into the countryside, so that produce could be brought into the markets. This reminds us that for the Romans, the town was made up of not only the central, built-up area but also the immediate countryside on which the town relied for its supplies.

Working Life in the Roman Town

Objects recovered at Wroxeter show that many trades were practised there. The most lucrative trades appear to have been related to domestic animals, especially cattle and sheep – a continuation of the farming practices of the Cornovii. When these animals were killed, nothing was wasted: the meat would have been sold in the market; the hides and fleeces would have been processed by leather workers and weavers; and the bones would have gone to the bone workers, whose debris has been found alongside bone pins and combs.

There is evidence of pottery and tile production, as well as the reworking of cullet (scrap glass), perhaps to make beads and bangles, and there is strong evidence too for metal brooch production and for iron smithing. Timber working both for houses but also for furniture would have been a vital industry, but little evidence has survived. Some trades were reliant on the import of

Above left: Third-century relief of a blacksmith's shop and tools
Above right: Roman bone pins found at Wroxeter
Below: A Roman bucket, made of iron and wood, found at Wroxeter

raw materials from elsewhere: gem cutters and shale and jet workers, for instance, used raw materials from the Continent, Dorset and Yorkshire.

Some of these trades would have been carried out in the workshops that can be seen lining the main roads, but others were concentrated in distinct parts of the town. Fulling and tanning, for example, were heavily dependent on water and involved the use of human and animal waste to process the hides. Trades such as this were often kept well away from the houses of the rich. Fire was also a notorious problem: evidence has been found of at least one devastating fire that swept across the northern half of the town, perhaps the same conflagration that burnt down the forum in about AD 170 (see page 17).

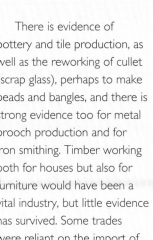

Right: A reconstruction drawing of Whitley Grange, a Roman hunting lodge just outside Wroxeter, which had a fine mosaic and large private bath house
Below: Bronze figure of the goddess Diana, found at Wroxeter

WROXETER'S HINTERLAND

Unusually for a Roman town in Britain we have a good understanding of the relationship between Wroxeter and its surroundings. A survey of the landscape around the site in the mid 1990s demonstrated that there were many farmsteads nearby but that these did not use many of the goods produced in or imported into the town. Instead, for most people in the countryside the existence of the town seems to have been an irrelevance, although there is clear evidence that the town had an impact on the local economy. Analysis of the farms immediately around the town showed they were located on soils more suitable for pasture than arable. Perhaps these farms were used to fatten up cattle before taking them to the livestock market, the *forum boarium*, which was apparently located at the highest point of the town, adjacent to its water supply.

The rich who lived in the town invested in property in the countryside by building villas. Only a handful of these have been found but they demonstrate clear growth during the third and fourth centuries. The best known is Whitley Grange, in the Rea Valley near Shrewsbury, built in the latter half of the fourth century. This appears to have been a hunting lodge rather than a Roman farm and had a fine mosaic and a large private bathhouse.

TRADE ROUTES

The road system was essential for trade. For example, the stone used to build the town was not transported by river but most likely by road; the red sandstone and coarse grey sandstone came from Ketley Bank, now in Telford; the fine-grained sandstone came from Hoar Edge, a quarry lying eight miles to the south of the town; and the limestone for the mortar came from Much Wenlock. All these sites are far from the river Severn.

Roman Religion

The Romans were tolerant of other religions, except where they conflicted with conventional Roman religious practice. They only banned the Druids, for example, because they were thought to practise human sacrifice. The Romans worshipped many gods, and worship was essentially a matter of personal choice. At least one house in Wroxeter was equipped with a shrine for the household gods (a *lararium*), where daily sacrifice was made to protect the house and home. Portable shrines have also been found.

There were a number of temples at Wroxeter but only one has been excavated, by Bushe-Fox between 1912 and 1913. The town's main temple perhaps lay at the principal crossroads and three other temples have been located by

aerial photography or geophysics. These consisted of a series of concentric walls with a tower-like central room (the *cella*) and a surrounding portico or ambulatory.

We do not know which gods were worshipped here but reliefs of Venus, Mercury (god of trade and prosperity) and Vulcan, the smith god, have been found. Normally, these gods were equated with equivalent native deities, allowing worship by Roman and native alike. Evidence has also been found for the worship of Jupiter in the form of an elaborately carved Jupiter column, a monument type common in northern Europe, especially in Germany, which may indicate the continuing influence of the army veterans, as the legions had come to

Above: A Roman capital carved with grapes and a hare, found at Wroxeter, reflecting the cult of Bacchus, Roman god of wine

Below: A small lead shrine of the goddess Venus, found at Wroxeter

Britain from bases in what is now Germany. Evidence of more exotic cults, such as the worship of Bacchus, which became more popular in the later Empire, has also been found in Wroxeter. A capital carved with grapes and a hare (see above), found in Wroxeter, reflects this cult.

Both the town's officials and its citizens would also have sacrificed to the emperor, in the hope that they would stay safe and healthy, and thus ensure everyone's well-being.

Right: A reconstruction drawing of Meole Brace roadside settlement. This was the nearest township to Wroxeter on the route into what is now Wales

Below: Colossal head of Constantine the Great (r.306–337), who was the first emperor to recognize Christianity

THE LATER ROMAN TOWN

By the end of the second century, all the major civic buildings in the town had been constructed, as had the defences. These cut off the fields surrounding the town and slightly reduced the area inside the walls. From what can be seen of the town through the geophysical survey, there was little open space, except perhaps in the southern part. Over 250 separate buildings have been found and many more have been traced in the geophysical survey but they cannot be identified without excavation. It is impossible to say what the town's population was in this period, as we cannot know how many people lived in each house, but perhaps between 5,000 and 10,000 people lived in Wroxeter in its heyday.

The third century saw a period of instability in the Empire, brought about by a succession of weak emperors who fought to establish their rule over a period of 50 years. This resulted in invasions and rampant inflation as the emperors tried to buy the loyalty of the army. This period affected Britain less than other parts of the Empire but resulted in long periods when Britain was not under Roman control. This was only fully re-established in AD 296 when Constantius I (Constantine the Great's father) captured Britain from the rebel Allectus.

The Roman Empire was profoundly changed by this instability and what emerged was a much more centralized and authoritarian regime with a powerful and influential army and civil service. To prevent such a crisis from reoccurring, the Emperor Diocletian (r.284–305) reformed the government and broke up the old provinces into much smaller ones. Britain was divided into four. Wroxeter was within Britannia Prima, whose capital was at Cirencester. This province encompassed the western part of Britain, including the south-west peninsula, Wales, and the Marches up to the Mersey. The recognition of Christianity by Constantine the Great in AD 313 was another seismic change: by the end of the century the Empire was officially Christian.

There is little sign of decline in Wroxeter in the third and fourth centuries but there was change. For those living in the west of Britain, the creation of a new province and capital increasingly shifted the focus of power away from London to Cirencester. The creation of a governor, his staff and the army who protected the new capital created opportunities for lucrative state employment that must have been very attractive for the elite of the province, from Wroxeter and elsewhere. To obtain positions, however, meant living at least part of the time in Cirencester and this might explain why there are so many villas there and around Gloucester.

Social and political links such as these explain why there are mosaics in and around Wroxeter that were apparently made by craftsmen from Cirencester. These mosaics were, however, paid for by individuals; the elite were no longer investing in repairing old civic structures but instead spent their money on themselves. This would have had serious consequences for the town's governance and finances, but even more catastrophic was the Empire-wide inflation that meant that the local taxes the town collected were increasingly worthless.

This lack of funds had an impact on the maintenance of the town. As the large civic buildings got older, it became more difficult to keep them going. Some money was spent on the baths in the early fourth century and on improving the defences, although work was kept to a minimum and expense was avoided. Parts of the forum appear to have been abandoned, perhaps in response to the decline in local government. The temples were abandoned by the end of the fourth century, by which time Wroxeter would have had a bishop, although it is not clear where his church was.

THE FIFTH AND SIXTH CENTURIES

The period between the collapse of Roman Britain, at some point in the early fifth century, and the emergence of the kingdoms of Anglo-Saxon England by the mid seventh century, is often referred to as the Dark Ages. It is a time associated with myths and legends and shadowy figures such as King Arthur. At Wroxeter, however, this period is remarkable for the lack of apparent change, at least initially. The end of Roman rule by the end of the first decade of the fifth century may not

Above: Gold aureus of the Emperor Diocletian (r.284–305), who divided Britain into four provinces
Below: A detail of the mosaic floor in Chedworth Roman Villa, Gloucestershire. This was one of many villas built around the new provincial capital at Cirencester, as the rich and powerful moved out of Wroxeter

Above: Fragments of a late Roman amphora originally from Gaza but found at Wroxeter, demonstrating extensive trade networks even at this late period

Right: Roman Britain was divided into four (later five) provinces. Wroxeter was in the province known as Britannia Prima, depicted here on a copy of the Roman document known as the Notitia Dignitatum

have been as disastrous as might be imagined. Britain had existed as a Roman province outside Roman control before, in the third century. Britannia Prima, in particular, proved remarkably resilient. It had considerable natural resources: mineral deposits of lead, tin, silver and gold, as well as fertile agricultural lands and extensive woodlands. It had direct communication routes with the Eastern Roman Empire (Byzantium), even after the Western Roman Empire ended in AD 476, via the western seaways connecting to the Atlantic coasts of France and Spain and from there to the Mediterranean. Its large and prosperous towns would initially have tried to carry on as normal; in Wroxeter the baths appear to have been used until the end of the fifth century. Large civic buildings such as baths, however, needed specialist skills to maintain them and there are increasing signs that such skilled people were no longer to be found. Another concern was defence. Although those running Britannia Prima were used to governing within their own province, they would have had to raise an army to protect themselves since the emperor recalled his troops at the beginning of the fifth century to defend the heart of the Empire. In order to raise an army to

Finds from Wroxeter

The excavations at Wroxeter have generated one of the largest collections of artefacts in Roman Britain. Work is continuing on these objects as they tell us a great deal about the trades practised in the town, and the trading networks that brought them to Wroxeter. They also tell us how people dressed, and how fashions changed.

People looked at the images of the emperor and his family on coins and would copy their appearance. Men would grow beards or shave, following the emperor's lead. Women would copy the often elaborate hairstyles of the rich. The Wroxeter mirror and the numerous hairpins found in the town would have been used in this way. Both men and women wore brooches in the early Empire. Bronzesmiths made brooches in many different styles and it was common in Britain to decorate these with coloured enamel. Study of the artefacts tells us that in the later period women changed their hairstyles, needing fewer pins, and that they wore more bracelets.

Above left: This third- or fourth-century Roman silver mirror, found at Wroxeter, is one of the finest ever found in the Empire
Above right: Second-century bronze and enamel brooches found at Wroxeter
Below: Late Roman bone portrait of a man, from Wroxeter

Above: A grave found by a road at Wroxeter. Burials were forbidden within the town, so it is likely that this dates from the time when Roman rule had broken down

Right: Reconstruction drawing of the possible bishop's house, a timber-framed structure built inside the remains of the baths basilica in the fifth or sixth century

defend themselves, the elite of Britannia Prima may well have raised their own militia: a *cohors Cornoviorum* is known to have been at South Shields at the end of the fourth century, showing that this scenario is not impossible. Yet there is also evidence for the employment of men from Ireland, presumably as mercenaries. A tombstone of an Irishman, Cunorix, dating from about AD 500, found at Wroxeter, seems to suggest that this was the case. Moreover, the presence of many Irish place names on the western coasts of Wales and Cornwall indicates extensive settlement by the Irish, perhaps in a deliberate attempt to protect the province from attack.

The collapse of Roman power led to a gradual decline in town life at Wroxeter and in the other towns in Britannia Prima. Direct communication and trade routes with the Empire were severed as the incoming Anglo-Saxons increasingly took hold of the rest of Roman Britain. Although the western trade route was still in existence, only a trickle of goods would have got through to Wroxeter from Cornwall or the Welsh coast, where this material was landed. Despite this, the town's markets seem to have functioned into the latest phases, presumably only selling local produce and, with the collapse of a coin economy, there would have been a return to barter. It is likely that the population of the towns would have rapidly declined as food resources became scarcer. Analysis of animal bones in these late levels demonstrates greater reliance on wild species rather than domestic animals.

Above: This tombstone of an Irishman named Cunorix, buried in about AD 500 at Wroxeter, may indicate the presence of Irish mercenaries at this time, drafted in to protect the province

Early Christian Wroxeter

Yet Wroxeter did not collapse altogether. Careful excavation of the uppermost levels in the baths basilica demonstrated a widespread reorganization of the former basilica, which had been taken down as a dangerous structure perhaps at the end of the fifth century. Selective demolition of the basilica's walls created enough building materials to make a large platform on which to construct a timber-framed building, similar to the modern villa built here in 2010. This impressive structure was surrounded by other houses, also built in the Roman style and to Roman measurements; one was even built of stone.

It was at this time that the unheated room of the by now disused baths, behind the Old Work, was perhaps converted into a chapel. The town's dead were buried in the ruined hypocaust surrounding the chapel – a sure sign that Roman town life had by this time largely collapsed, since burial within the town walls was not permitted under Roman law. The possible construction of a chapel hints that the owner of the large building, who was clearly powerful enough to build it, could have been a cleric, probably Wroxeter's bishop. The phenomenon of late Roman bishops protecting and reorganizing town centres in the fifth century is known from the Continent but is very rare in Britain.

Quite when Wroxeter was abandoned as a town is unknown but it could have been in the mid sixth century when a great plague is known to have swept through western Britain, killing King Maelgwyn of Gwynedd, according to the Welsh Annals. Such an event might have had a devastating effect on a centre of population such as Wroxeter. Alternatively, the town may have been abandoned when the region fell to the pagan Anglo-Saxon King Penda of Mercia in the 650s, since the king had little sympathy with the British Church or with a surviving Roman town. It is possible that a small British monastery survived, located in the village.

SAXON AND MEDIEVAL WROXETER

Although the town of Viriconium failed, not everyone abandoned the site and the memory of the community there was preserved in an Anglo-Saxon document known as the Burghal Hidage, which records the service the Mercian king expected of different communities under his rule. One of the groups is called the 'Wreconsaete', the people of Wroxeter (or the Wrekin, although there is no evidence that people were living in the old Iron Age hillfort at that time).

A settlement persisted around the ford, perhaps originating in a small British monastery founded while the town still survived. The evidence for this comes from the impressive Anglo-Saxon church and associated sculpture. Fragments of a limestone cross shaft with figures can be seen in the south wall of the church. Dating from the time of King Offa (r.757–96) this was once a tall and impressive feature that served as a preaching cross. In Offa's time, such sculpture tended to be reserved only for the most important churches and monasteries. The north wall of the church is clearly Anglo-Saxon, perhaps dating from the 10th or 11th century. The

Above: Sculpture of a dog on the outside of the church, dating from the time of King Offa in the late eighth century

Below: The late Elizabethan alabaster effigies of Sir Richard Newport and his wife, Margaret, in St Andrew's Church. He was one of the queen's counsel for the Marches of Wales during the reign of Elizabeth I (r.1558–1603)

Church of St Eata in the neighbouring village of Atcham dates from the same time but is even better preserved.

We know from Domesday Book that at the time of the Conquest there were three priests serving at Wroxeter's church – a large number for what was then a rural parish. Similarly, the medieval parish of Wroxeter was highly unusual in crossing the river Severn, the division between the ancient dioceses of Lichfield and Hereford. This anomaly might have come about through the survival of Wroxeter's *territorium*, the area owned by the town that provided the resources to maintain it. This could have happened if the *territorium* had been gifted to the Church in the Anglo-Saxon period.

The Normans also considered Wroxeter important. The Fitz Alan family held the manor from the mid 12th century and built a manor house in a field opposite the church, remodelling the defences to create fishponds. They paid to extend the church, as shown by the surviving fine chancel, and they arranged for Haughmond Abbey to take care of the parish. The church reached the peak of its size in the 14th century but after that the village declined.

Above: Thomas Telford, the civil engineer, who recorded the excavation of a Roman house at Wroxeter in 1788
Below: A map of Wroxeter drawn by John Rocque in 1746, showing the medieval fields before they were swept away

ANTIQUARIAN INTEREST

Antiquarian interest in Wroxeter is first recorded in the 16th century. John Leland visited Wroxeter during Henry VIII's reign. He was recording the possessions of the Crown, including the remains of the ruined abbeys and monasteries, as well as more ancient sites. He describes the Old Work and the defences at Wroxeter, revealing that nothing more of the site survived then than was visible in the Victorian period. A traveller writing in 1743 noted that 'the peasantry of the place have generally some of these coins for sale … they are locally called dinders, a word no doubt corrupted from the Latin denarius'. In this the locals were carrying on an old tradition: a 13th-century court case saw two men brought to the manorial court charged with searching for treasure on the lord's land. Many stories were told about how the town had vanished. The most colourful said that a flock of sparrows carried the town away one night in their beaks. Clearly nothing was known of the town and even its name had been forgotten.

In the 18th century, curiosity about the site grew as fashionable young aristocrats started visiting the Continent to see ancient sites. These 'Grand Tours' sparked an interest in

Remains of Urice near Wroxeter 1700 outside

Britain's classical past. By then the town had been divided between two estates: the Berwick estate at Attingham Park and the Raby estate of the Earls of Bradford. A map created by John Rocque in 1746 records the medieval open fields of ridge and furrow just before they were swept away by enclosure hedges. By this time a turnpike road had already been cut diagonally across Wroxeter, taking traffic from Shrewsbury to the forges at Leighton and Coalbrookdale. By the end of the 18th century, the road went as far as Iron Bridge – the world's first cast-iron bridge and the new technological wonder. In 1788, the county engineer, Thomas Telford, recorded in meticulous detail a Roman house with heated rooms uncovered at Wroxeter. Researchers soon identified the site as the town of Uriconium, listed in a Roman document known as the 'Antonine Itinerary', but there was no proof of the ancient name of the site.

Above: Remains of Uriconium near Wroxeter, 1788, by the Revd Williams

Below: One of the buildings of the model farm in the centre of Roman Wroxeter, begun in 1854

Above: A view of Wroxeter by Thomas Prytherch, painted soon after the baths were uncovered in 1859
Below: Portrait of Charles Dickens by William Powell Frith. Dickens visited Wroxeter on 14 May 1859 and left a detailed account of his time there

EARLY EXCAVATIONS

The coming of the railway to Shropshire revolutionized access to Wroxeter. Early antiquarian visitors from London could now visit more easily and they recorded the discoveries made by the villagers. The London-based antiquarian Thomas Wright, whose family lived in Ludlow, persuaded the local MP Beriah Botfield to assist him in raising funds to excavate at Wroxeter. Work began in February 1859 and Wright had spectacular success in uncovering the remains of the baths, which were still standing to an impressive height. Visitors flocked to see the site, including miners from Cannock on a day trip and the author Charles Dickens, who left a vivid account of his visit.

Wright continued to excavate at the site until 1867. It was such a popular visitor attraction that the Earl of Bradford donated it to the Shropshire Archaeological Society; they looked after the ruins for the next 90 years, maintaining a custodian and a museum there. Thomas Wright was not a great excavator but he was a superb publicist. His lurid account

Dickens on Wroxeter
'There is a bright spring morning over head, the old wall standing close by looks blank at us; here and there a stray antiquary clambers among the rubbish, careless of dirt stains; an attentive gentleman on the crest of a dirt heap explains Roman antiquities to some young ladies in pink and blue, who have made Wroxeter the business of a morning drive. An intelligent labourer, who seems to be a sort of foreman of the works, waits to disclose to the honorary secretary the contents of a box in which it is his business to deposit each day's findings of small odds and ends …'

of Wroxeter's demise in fire and flames, complete with bodies abandoned in the hypocaust of the baths, inspired the work of local artist Thomas Prytherch. One of his paintings (now at Kenilworth Castle) records a peaceful view of the ruins; the other depicts the fall of Uriconium (see page 24).

By this time, however, the village was in decline. The creation of a model farm by the Raby estate in the centre of Wroxeter from 1854 had a significant impact on the village. The estate provided workers' cottages next to the farm and in the village. Most of the agricultural population of the village lost their land and work and had moved out before the first Ordnance Survey map of the village was made in 1880. This trend was repeated all over England as agriculture was mechanized.

'At Viricon today
The village anvil rests on
Roman base'
(Wilfred Owen, *Uriconium:
An Ode*, c.1913)

THE 20TH CENTURY

Further excavations were carried out on a field north of the village by the Inspector of Ancient Monuments, JP Bushe-Fox, between 1912 and 1914. Among the students who assisted in this excavation was the archaeologist Sir Mortimer Wheeler who, in his autobiography, recalled that of all the students working with him, he was the only one to return from the Western Front in the First World War. These excavations uncovered the remains of a number of houses and a small temple, inspiring the poet Wilfred Owen to write an ode that noted the touching remains of everyday life.

AE Housman may also have visited at a slightly earlier date since his famous poem, *A Shropshire Lad*, records the melancholy of the abandoned town ('To-day the Roman and his trouble/Are ashes under Uricon'). A third poet, Mary Webb,

Above: The poet Wilfred Owen, who lived near Wroxeter and visited the excavations

Below: JP Bushe-Fox's excavations of the temple at Wroxeter in 1913

Above: *View of the recreated town house, looking towards the Church Stretton gap, where the Roman road led to Gloucester and Caerleon*

visited in the 1920s to see the remains of the forum excavated by Professor Donald Atkinson of the University of Manchester, when the town's name was revealed in the forum inscription (see page 32).

At the same time, the first aerial photographs were taken of the ruins showing their poor condition. During the Second World War the site was closed to the public and a searchlight battery team was stationed here, protecting Atcham airfield a mile to the north. An unfortunate legacy of the airfield was that in the immediate post-war period, local farmers borrowed the bulldozers from the American base to level the ramparts within the town, before the town was protected by legislation.

The State acquired the ruins in 1947 and began putting the site into better order. Archaeological discoveries continued apace through the aerial surveys of Arnold Baker and others and the archaeological excavations, conducted by Graham Webster and Philip Barker of the University of Birmingham, on the baths site. Once the site had been consolidated by the 1990s, work was carried out by Birmingham University working with English Heritage and Geophysical Surveys of Bradford to create the first geophysical survey of an entire Roman town in Britain. This work still continues intermittently, although the results of the first major survey are now published. The findings from this survey have doubled the number of known buildings in the town to over 250 and demonstrate that large parts of the town were intensively occupied. This work continues to show the importance of non-invasive archaeology at Wroxeter, the results of which are revolutionizing our picture of this site without damaging it.